When a poem speaks

DuDu

EVERSPRING PUBLISHING

When a Poem Speaks

COPYRIGHT 2018 by Dudu (Zhanqing Du)

ISBN 978-1-7751288-5-4
ISBN 1-7751288-5-7

Printed in the U.S.A
This edition first printing, June 2018

This is a collection of Zhanqing Du's English poems. Names,
characters, places, and incidents are the product of the author's
creativity. And any resemblance to actual persons, living or dead,
businesses, companies, events, or locales might be coincidental.

Zhanqing Du, well-known for her pen name "*Dudu*", is a female Chinese Canadian writer. She has been a longtime serialized novel writer and column writer in two Chinese newspapers "Ottawa China News" and "Ottawa Weekend". She possesses a wide prospective and deeper understanding of diversity and connections on culture between the East and the West. Dudu is a member of Association of Overseas Female Writers in Chinese Literature, a member of Canadian Chinese Writers' Association, and a member of Chinese Pen Society of Canada.

Her published books in Chinese include:

- "The Grassland" - collected proses and short fictions,
- "Dudu from the End of the World" - a collection of proses, available in Taobao.com, dangdang.com
- "The Song of Four Seasons Behind the Glass Wall" - a poetry anthology,
- "Days without Potatoes" - a collection of novels, (Amazon.com)
- "Emma in Rose" - a collection of short stories, (Amazon.com)
- "The Chess of God"- a collection of poems, (Amazon.com)
- "A Road Heading to Sky" - a collection of proses (Amazon.com)
- "One bookmark"-a collection of poems

Dudu has won various honors and awards in Chinese literature over the years, including:

- First Place in Fiction, American Hanxin Literature Award;
- Best Novel in Fiction, Taiwan Lin Yu-Tang Literature Award;
- First Place in Poetry, Canadian Chinese Writer's Award;
- Second Place in non-fiction(prose), American Hanxin Literature Award;
- Second Place in non-fiction(prose), Overseas Chinese Creative Writing Award.
- And many more other literary awards

Dudu holds a Bachelor degree of Laws from Shanxi University, China. She also studied Social Psychology at the University of Helsinki, Finland, and Software Program Design, at the University of Ottawa, Canada. Besides a writer, Dudu is also an owner of a beauty salon, and an Aqua fittness instructor. She lives in Ottawa, Ontario, Canada.

Enthusiastic and optimistic, *Dudu* is a writer who believes in that love is the basis of life. She values her family in the first place. Apart from a wide range of hobbies, such as sports, singing, culinary art, knitting, apparel design, gardening, and painting etc, she also enjoys volunteering in community activities and events. Down-to-earth attitude gives her strength to face anything in life. She likes to describe herself as a small fish full of freedom, enjoying happily the calm of the ocean, as well as fighting bravely against the tempest. She regards the free spirit as the tip of hierarchy in life.

Dudu's email address: zhanqingdu@yahoo.com
Facebook page: https://www.facebook.com/zhanqing.du
Twitter page: https://twitter.com/zhanqingdu
Wechat ID: butterflydudu

for people I love

You make my empty life full

CONTENTS

A dream under your pillow

Hide myself under your pillow
I breathe a promise
Stay as close as I can
To your dream

I might laugh, when
You win
I might cry, when
You sigh
Shout, to wake you up
When you are in fear

Won't go far, I am
near

If you don't remember
The moment, when eyes
Open, flip your pillow
I am here

A poem for Dr.C

If I'm allowed to borrow a poem
I would ask it speaking to you
You will wake up from discomfort
Start laughing under bright light

If there are notes in this poem
I would sing soprano for you
Your eyes will open
And wow to the happy melody

If this poem has feet
I would dance Flamenco and circle you
You will get up and join me
In a inky black night

If Chinese characters make a pool
in this poem
I would invite you swim with me
The warmth and softness you feel
Like a spring breeze under the sky

If a poem is an almighty doctor
I would beg him to take care of you
Just like what you did to us
Day by day, year after year
The love will never dry

If there was a "thanks" hiding in the poem
I want to enlarge it to Infinity
And watch it fly, fly and fly

No matter how poor words are
To express love and appreciation
We still need to use them
For boundless wishes, to erase sighs

For your health and happiness
"Doctor, don't be a patient."
A voice from the bottom of our hearts:
"Have a good rest and get well soon
Tomorrow, let's all be high!"

After soaking in a pool

Soaked in a pool of cheers
Surrounded by announcement, applause
Gazing, greetings, wine, smiles
And waves from vibrating hearts

I live in a dream
In daytime

Many days pass
News is new no more.
A true story in a dream
Still true, but
Dreams are never real

A wakeup call ringing
On the other end of the month
A picture of impressionistic strokes
Start whispering：
Come in, come in

Standing in the middle of the mist

In the frame,

A woman holds her books

Bright smiles shining

Hairs hanging long

A black waterfall

So black like night

Without moon and stars

Moon and stars, and the sun

Are all

In her heart

Naked snow

Poems hide in snow

Out of the windows and along the road

If you want to dig them out

Your warm heart should shine on the top

Melt the snow with your enthusiasm

There in front of you

Naked poems are everywhere

Fifty is a Start

Fifty is a start
For a life has been filled with
People, animals and passion
A road of experience becomes a past
I believe, in Lisa's fashion
Future is a big smile of expression

Fifty is a start
For a heart of love
That knows how to give
People around you feel the heat
I believe, in Lisa's perspective
Kindness is something primitive

Fifty is a start
For a family of three
Carrying a harmony of peace
When the cute, green car leaves
I believe, in Lisa's masterpiece
Together, you are having a great feast

Fifty is a start

For Brian, Amy, neighbours and friends

You are a morning sun

Penetrating the darkness

You are a breeze

Blowing off a hat of sadness

You are a little eraser

Erasing the soreness

You are a rainbow, after the rain

Colouring the sky of wilderness

Fifty is a start

Work, like you always do

Happy, even when you feel blue

Love, like a hot fondue

Oh, Lisa you will do

Fifty is a start

I give this as a gift to you

To show the love from our heart

Please take it and

Let it on your way to spark

Spark and spark

Happy 50 Birthday to dear Lisa

You

You are the red wind from far
Half sky covered by your love
Look at the mirror under your feet
Your dimples trembling in those ripples
Like Shimmery stars

You are a sky after a rain
An island free of train, a family
Of fish and birds, a bed
Of trees and peace, a dream
Of moonlight and harmony, a soul
Of clear water
Without human stain

You are a myth standing there
Smile to the world without any fear
Past and tomorrow are not on your list
Together with all members of your family
You love, you love with cheer
Today, today is here

When a poem speaks

When a poem speaks
A dictionary is not a must
The only ruler is your heart
To measure definitions and doubts
Pain and gain, right or wrong
Past and present, black or white

When a poem speaks
A question is an answer
One word on screen
Two behind, maybe three, or four
Even ten, a hundred, a million
On the way, invisible

When a poem speaks
Still life becomes animated
Animated thoughts frozen
In a line, or in a word
Unbreakable beauty
Sits between lines
Your heart is the solution

To decode the empty space

If a poem can talk
Let it talk his own dialect
If a poem can sing
Let it sing her own notes
If a poem is willing to answer
It already has its own marker
A cross, a check or a blank

When you dig too deep
You'll miss trees, grass and flowers,
Houses, people, and dogs around
When you focus the underneath
You won't feel the breeze, the sun
The mist, the color surrounds

Be simple
The hardest language to learn
To tell the truth
Stay on the surface is the best way
To see more, and feel more

3 o'clock

It's 3 am
How many souls
Stay in awaken senses
How much love
Hides in perfect dreams
How much pain
Faints away in subconscious insomnia
How much recovery
Gained in this dark silence

Thousands of angers
Calmed down in this moment
Hundreds of burns
Sealed under the blanket

And love, to people and the world
And hate, to past and today
And regret, to you and me
Suspends for now and tomorrow
Tons of agonies

Disappear in even-breathing

Only me
Eyes open widely
Mind walking wildly
With everything above
Lively

You are a beautiful seed

You are a beautiful seed
Sowed in an ordinary morning
Field will be covered by your leaves
A limping girl will run and laugh
Fruits filling her basket
Harvest is at the end
If there is no fruit to pick up
It's not the end

You are a beautiful seed
Sowed in an autumn morning
An implanted ligament will build a bridge
Connect an old me and a new you
Fruit is the walking steps
Without hesitations
A blown knee becomes new
Without two-side effects
Doctor and patient
Life won't be full of juicy trees

You are a beautiful seed

Sowed in a body not young

A hope will appear in 6 month

That's the time of drinking wine

Grapes will hang on the vine

Without regret

A pair of new legs can jump to reach

The biggest grape

A collection online

A life of love and pain in miniature
Built with words and rhythms
Forming a flossy version
of affections and existence

Whispering gently
about a back shadow, an unknown future
and a present you with generous sentiments

One click log in, show starts
One click log out, life begins

A patient in bed

Work no more
Everybody starts working for you
Worry no more
Everybody starts worrying about you
Taking care of others no more
Everybody starts taking care of you

Things are in the other way around
When you are not able to get up and be strong

Zero task is waiting
Hurry no more
Time is like an empty room in your front
White spaces to be filled with free mind
Bright sunbeam drops a shining spot on bed
Bouncing back with unpredictable thoughts

You may think, or not think
Recall old days, or just ignore them
Imagine, or just pretend you are
Dream your dream

Create a new one and forget the bad one

She talks gently with gold wishes
You don't need to earn it with effort
He treats you patiently with cloud- like gentle
hands
You don't need to ask for it
They tolerate your temper
You don't need to feel guilty
Love, filled your space directly without hiding
The reason is what you just lost----Health

Sickness is a hidden treasure
Buried under a healthy body
Shines brightly
When it's been discovered
A wealthy person suddenly born
With luxury resting and countless time
Comfortable like a lazy queen
With food you dream to eat
And you are free of cooking and cleaning
With floral surrounding
You became Flora the Goddess of Roman myth
In bed, eyes are brighter than

Standing on the ground
You see things bigger and prettier
In a horizontal angle
Even something you never saw
Is hoping, chatting and sparkling

You see
Sickness is a gift of life
Makes you rich of feeling love, and
Stops you from struggling for daily life

It's the music waking up
Your sleepy senses of appreciation
It's time to count how much luck in life

Show your teeth to life when you are sick
For those hidden love
Be proud to be a temporary queen
Be rich to own a palace of love

It's a short period when you are sick
But, what you just realized
Will stay long

A day when there is freezing rain

Crystal window on the east wall

Millions reflex light shines away

Outside

Ice covered a shining white world

Inside

Mother and daughter cuddling in bed

Curled

Appear, and disappear

You appear, you disappear
One end extended from the land far east
Another end located west in my heart

Walking over Pacific Ocean
Two cultures connected

You arrive in one insomnia night
Visiting a shaking soul

You appear, you disappear
Distance appears, Distance disappears

Note: Sometimes, I don't know how to identify myself. A woman living in western country with a Chinese heart? No, when I visit China, I am a western woman with a Chinese face. An invisible mixture of culture confused me. And the feeling enlarges in an insomnia night.

Big bang of love

It explodes
A basic of everything
Different forces emerged after
Sun shines, wind blows, water flows and trees
grow
Life starts a new picture
Love fits in
No matter what's in front

An old galaxy shattered into pieces
A new one opened instead
Everything begins from nothing
Nothing is as rich as everything
Seasons needed
To form a plant from a seed
Life needs to grow tall from a fetus
Time, let time talk in love
Years, let years walk along love

When an unexpected love from nowhere
comes to you

Everywhere changes

Million pieces of residue

flow in the galaxy of a heart

No explanation

It's the Big Bang

Everlasting will be expected

Soul digger

I read you in bed
Wrapped warm and still
A butterfly ready to hatch
In air and on ground
Spirit flies with wings of ecstatic dream
Body kneels down to worship a sparkle flame
Something going up, up, and up high
Something digging down, down, and down low

You, smile in lines and lines
True feelings filling my blood and pillow
"Love, there is no up and down, right or wrong"
You say, you behave, you write,
you sing a love song
Passing 600 years, a mythical giant is still alive
In my hand and eyes, in my room and heart
Shining blaze emits around
In the morning shadow

A soul digger

Wakes me up soundlessly

My only choice is:

Swallow and follow

A story in autumn

The tail of summer hiding in a breeze

Blows hope into autumn

Crosses my heart and your heart

Hanging on the tip of a tree

Light faints from east to west

Night awakes an owl and a bat

In the circle of their eyes

Flowers cover dirt, howling is musical

Even a waking bee stings spirit

Everything is pain free

You see nothing in the dark

Doesn't mean the world's gone

Using an eye in the heart

I look down at the river in dim dawn

A smile in the whirl of the wave

Hugging and nagging all around

Stone stands, water flows, leaves follow

It goes with time without a "So long"

On tip of the tree

Dreams are always random and agree

Tigers shaking hands with rabbits

Snakes giving sweet kisses to mice

Nothing needs a referee

A story in this autumn

Is turning a page top to bottom

End the ordeal in body and mind

Start a future of soft and lively hum

A heart of rain

Suddenly, rain falls
Gone with the unbearable drought
Every drop rings a note
Touches the leaves, touches skin
Touches the soil, touches soul
On the grass in yellow
In the thirst of hearts
A soprano has been heard

Patience is your weapon
Whispering in yesterdays' wind
Expectation is my companion
Low as grass under feet
Today, today is another day
Hope, stores in a tomorrow
There will be a nice painting with sunflowers
Since Van Gogh is part of a heart
Never die, hope
Never dry, desire

A heart of rain lives

In one single drop of tear

One, adds up to thousands

Thousands, come from one

Roundabout

Exits, stretching out from the heart of an octopus
Every single tentacle
Leads towards a designed destiny
With different trees along the side
Different houses built in different times, and
People in the houses carry different hearts

Left arm won't able to stay straight
and reach right arm
When your desire turns to the right one
Your left one has to bend and curve around
No short cut in front

Roundabout is all about exit in a Round
Without the Round, no way to be out
A way to go further
Starts from a nice Round

When you found you are in a wrong direction
Back to the Roundabout
Going one more round, maybe another one

A solution presents

Be a part of the center of a maze
Means you are facing more ways

Sometimes, going back
And bending your heart and body
Is the first step
Of moving forward

As a Chinese idiom describes:
"You can bend or unbend!"
Just like you may bow and rise at will

Day and night

If a night should be dark
It's bright at the moment
You are a fire burning hard
Lightening up my sky with blaze
Darkness lost a war
Day, wins

If a day should be filled with time-clicking sound
It's now silent like an old rusty clock
You are the irremovable rust
Ceased the farther clicks
Everything stops in an era
of imaginary battle of love

When a heart surrendered
Day is not a day
Night is not a night
Time freezes in a game of two
I doubt about my identity
You wonder "who is who"
In a river of love

Consciousness gone with whispering:

No discipline, no rules

No day, no night

Doubt and draught

End of a draught summer
Rain came pouring
Thirsty ground drinking madly
Sucking hard and thorough wildly
Yellow grass turning to green velvet
Flowers blooming out millions of colors
Butterflies flying in the love garden
Quivering and gentle, a breeze sings:
Rain, rain, rain
Where have you been
Am I your final destiny
Hold all your passions in

Rivers start interrupting
Come on, rain
I can take you to the sea
You may flow in my arms
Lakes join in
Be smart, rain
You belong to my pond

Don't follow a wrong wand
Stream laughing loudly
Rain, rain, rain
Forever and always
You are my fond

You came from the clouds
Own a home of the whole sky
A choice in your treasure dream box
Can be rivers, lakes and streams
Even become a piece of green
Hiding in the grass

I am the dust under the grass
If you are the rain
If I am the dry ground
What is your answer
My rain, rain, rain

How

How many words have gone through the wires
How much trust has grown from seeds to flowers
How many meals on a narrow seat served
without a burning candle
How many miles has covered under a fleece
blanket
How many underwears colored the date of a birth
How much happiness a love has produced

Thousands of "How"s waiting to be answered
How you touch me, suck me, chew me, and stab
me
How you miss me, dream me, think me, and
worry me
How we start, we suffer, we agree, we argue, we
suffer, and win

Look at the hair missing in the middle of your
scalp
Look at the wrinkles crawling around my eyes

Look at the easiness when we sit together doing
nothing
Look at the hardship when distance
stands and stares
Our thoughts fly through air,
our bodies travel within time
Sparkles burning in your eyes, lighting up a fire in
my heart
Passing day and night, linking spring and autumn
Two souls merged in one like a bug
and a stone in a fossil
Name an inerasable history of two

No questions needed, no answers exist
Being ourselves and being true
is an recorded today

Swimming in a pool of "How"s
is just a game of cross-word when we doubt
You say: stop asking, start enjoying

No matter what styles under our strokes
We are both champion of the pool

Outside the reptile zoo

Crickets laughing in the bush
Mother sitting in a car with open windows
Wordless voices traveling around
From a baby in a cradle, tender and quiet
To a big you with black Rapunzel hair
Dancing in wind

Big is a wrong word in this giant world
It is a precise form in my arm
Love, stores in my hugs and never goes far
No matter how tall you grow
No matter how old I become

Mind floating against you and me
Baby, my little pacific snake
Always sings a hissing song
Low and soft, shy and holds on
Never complains and shouts out, even
Your grief becomes river of tears flowing long

Your tenderness is as strong as

a layer of sticky tar

Crawling over your age alone a 10 years passed

Lengthen those wrinkles on my forehead

Erasing your innocence like a dim star

hiding under sun

How many years will we stay with you?

Wind whispers: It's as short as your lovely blink

Holding your hands in the zoo

Daddy drowned his heart in your laughter

Touching your happiness in the car

Mommy reviewed a story of you with a tear just

start

A Saturday afternoon on September the first

Sky is pure blue, leaves are still green

I put a poem of you in my cup

Drink it slowly in an open-window car

Shield

Experience of life turned into a shield
When Cupid fired an arrow through ages
Can't return a heart with the arrow on
Love behind the shield has to yield

History of a person turned into a shield
When an old friend arrived like a new
Shall I expose a bright smile without hesitation?
Love behind the shield uncontrollably paled

Members in life turned into a shield
When a north leave getting a shine
from a south sun
Where can I bury the path covered by maple
foliage?
Love behind the shield has to be piled

Responsibility turned into a shield
When mind travels free in a story of two
How to conquer the storm without any damage?
Love behind the shield has to be nailed

If a shield is not made of unbroken steel
If your spear like a passing tornado
If no more experience,
history,member and responsibility
Will the solid land of free love survive through
Whatever, whenever, however and forever?

Sadly announced in a voice of heaven:
Children, there is no IF in life

Walking in an invisible love
is making an narrow only path
towards another heart
Shield stays, behind its dull face
Laugh and cry, sleep and awake, wet and dry
Leading to an unclear day of tomorrow, and
Many unclear days after tomorrow

A battle of two winners

Wake up in midnight
Out of a burning dream
Leaves of the tall tree were on fire
Like a million hot tongues licking together
Lighting a pitch dark night in butterfly valley

I see a queen of desire sitting naked in the valley
Pickled by juicy semen, silky skin
Like silk just came out of a silkworm, sticky
When the tree shakes and moves

Her red mouth turned into a whirl pool
Sucked everything deep deep in

Tight as a python's squeeze to a mouse
Smooth as water surface without winkles
Firm as an old tree rooted a hundred meters
deep
Wet as a melting river in early spring
Sing as a lark twittering in love

Thy stem and trunk drowned into her pool

No mercy to let the tree escape

Both melting, willingly,

Crazy to death

Disappeared, a queen and a king

When flames within

Burned to ashes, the war

Finally has an ending after ten seasons long

A battle finished with a compromise

reached by both sides before it begins

Winners are two:

A queen of desire, and a tree of king

A dancer

Run in the rain storm of mind
Dance in the lines of words
The whole street made of bricks of passion
Every single dance step
located on a key of an organ
Music flowed in autumn air
Windows opened to burst out cheer
A stage for her is always there

Love came upon,   if you don't believe
Touch her pointing feet covered by dried blood
Taste the salty tears dripping from her heart
Listen to the notes jumping in her lines
Look at the river of words flooding
in her sleepless night

A dancer's joy came from love of dance
Without words, without lines
Her love has nowhere to go
Let her love, let her go

Let Lines extend to sky high with no end

Let words carry time to future land

A dancer is dancing

In an imaginary street

She is the wealthy builder

owns infinite lines and words

More streets will be there

A city of poetry will be near

In the puzzle

Many paths, crossing my mind
Leads to various directions of many kinds
Where to go? I wondered
Crowds cried out loud at the dead end
Some giggling and laughing
They face an open land

Winter shines in snow
Summer sings in a river's flow
Do you see a snowflake in a hot summer day?
Can a sound from south beach
echoes in north bay?
Diversity differs each way

Either die from endless steps, or
Repeat in a wrong path a hundred times
Walking in a puzzle land makes a dangerous day
When you think you've found a way
The true exit is still far away

You know there is an exit, without guide
Somewhere has shining lights, can't hide
Like a real hope in real life
Not in a dream, seeing the other perfect half

A land full of uncertain steps requires love
Cost of your life and my life, may be tough
I don't escape, facing an unknown end
Be me when I was, I am and I will be
In love

Walking in a mystery
Makes a life-long history

Lost in the puzzle, looking at the sky
If I need to choose a way to try
I will say: Fly

Desire

I walk along the river bank
A thirsty mosquito dancing around
Sucking deep in me to get drunk
Desire is your uncontrollable hunt

You shine on the sandy beach
Pale color from north like bleach
Naked under you without a shadow
Desire is my darken skin you reach

You drop from high in a hot summer day
Cracking earth begging you stay
Getting wet is not a silly play
Desire is this only dream of rain on the way

You are a key of a prison door
Free me is what you are waiting for
I stare at the iron railing through a dark night
Desire is the footsteps carrying the key,
come closer

and closer, knocking the floor

Outside the iron door, temptation walks

Inside a heart, desire runs

A marathon between blocks

Wine and love

Holding a glass, shaking it gently
A drinker's smile colored the wine
Crimson glimmering inside, and outside on
cheeks
In, beam of her eyes lightly stirring the liquor
Out, a sensitive heart seeking love

"Thanks for giving me!" She whispered
A grateful chant echoed around
Enough is enough, inside out and outside in
Live an ordinary life
Is equally fun, if there is love

Sun shines on you, and also on me
Lights pour on gold, and also on rocks
Rain beats leaves and also dirts
Balance in time and space

We live, never skipped any yesterday
Won't miss any today and tomorrow
Love stays somewhere

Ready to give
Patiently, in a unseen shadow

She thanks for she can thank
Like this chalice of wine, Lucky to be drunk
And we are lucky for we are able to drink

Wine and drinker reached a deal
Be together, both fulfilled a meaning to heal
Turning the chalice, she smiled to the liquor
Whispered : "No no no,
I am not drunk! It is real."

All the coloured liquid went inside now, glass is
Empty, desire burning in her stomach
In mind, a voiceless song is echoing:
"In love, we survive.
I cannot live, without love."

Life's going on, one chalice
Finished, another one fills in
Just like, love

An ordinary her in an ordinary night

Wine and love, colored her cheeks and glass

A night before Thanksgiving

Sneaked by, she slept on

A fluffy couch, along

In dream, she hugs him

An only love

Chalice slipped off her hand

Fell on the carpet end

With no sound

Swim in poetry

Recently, I am addicted to swim
in water, and in poetry

Here, I open this window
swim like wind
cross mind and soul

Soaked in poetry
words are my fins
lines are the marks waving tail left

From this bank to
that bank, I swam
when I arrived, I found there
was another end in front

A cloudy morning

A purse, a hat, a malfunctioned pancreas
A pair of tireless legs, a handwriting address
A 75 years life experience in another land
A perfect tongue without English
A tube of glucose tablet
A phone, a longing heart filled with learning
desire
A piece of bread, a library as destination

You went in a cloudy morning, by
Bus, taking my heart with you
Many years ago, you did the same thing
Carry me everywhere in your womb

My body at home becomes a butterfly in stomach
Fly from windows to doors, from childhood to
now
Wings brush the glass of a memory box so clean
I saw your back shadow sewing my clothes
under a dim light
When I open my sleepy eyes

I hear cold water runs your hands, you are
rinsing my dress
Wrinkles crawl on your hands day by day
Rougher and rougher year by year
Until I am big like another you
Memory plays a film when time flows

Clock clicks, 10 minutes passed
30 minutes, 1 hour, 2 hours
Butterfly becomes a hungry lion
My pray is the ringing sound of
The phone or the doorbell
Come back, mom, come back
Please

Off at wrong stop?
Blood sugar getting low?
Faint in street?
Accident? Robbery?
Safe, are you safe?

I wish the whole city is only my house big
Finding you only need a few steps
I wish voice may travel like light

One second, you heard my clear call
I wish your heart linked with my heart
You worry when you feel that I worry

Torture is in every second
I am an ant on the stove top
Dancing with every single muscle

Love on Valentine's day

Love is air
Fills in everywhere
Around you and around me
With no reason and no despair

Love is a war
Between night and dawn
Weak and strong
Floating in our heart and will never drown

Love is worry
For how much I may share
And how much you may carry
Dream has an ending with pains to bury

Love is sweet
Your words are my candies
My words are your treat
For the words are lighting
The road under our feet

Love is funny
When you notice my smile
And when I see you happy
Your joy is my joy
Makes my day sunny

Love in Valentine's Day
Is an answer on the long way
Hot as burning the dried hay
Muzzling like a kiss without a say

"I love you" is a bunch of roses
Enchanting my dream
"You love me" is a card
Leading to your heart

Love is love
No true no false
Hold it gently like a baby dove
Unlock its wings free
For the ocean blue sky above
"I love you" is a fact
On St Valentine's Day for you to have

Pumpkin

Part of you is hollow

Used to be filled pitch dark and no shadow

My carving knife disclosed your desire

Pieces cutting off,

Candle lights shine in pair

Kneeled down shaping you into a legend

In dark, you play a solo of Phantom

No "trick or treat" disappoints in this sphere

Solitude

An afternoon trip on wheels one city to another
memory flow
Youth to wrinkles, dreams to reality,
hopes to bubbles, polluted grey sky to red maple
forest
A Chinese soul inhaling Canadian air
Stop wondering , stop asking time and mind
Roots, the answers hiding somewhere in united
universe

Haiku collection

White cover seals up the world

temperature underneath

is as deep as a heart

Morning laziness

muscle aching

an excuse for a blank mind

Many years later
I walk into the garden of
peace and quietness
the cost is restless youth

Sounds of wheels pressing the road
are loud enough
to enlarge solitude inside the car

Time has been edited
the fourth book
will talk

Jet-lagged love
his sleep
wakes me up

Seepless night

pain wakes up from a conversation with XN

the dearest is the loveless

A tree tip out there

carries my floating heart

clear window in front

divides body and mind

You see more

with your ear, heart and feeling

a life in melody

inspires a dream girl

Ski Vorlage on the way

destiny is the tip of your heart

and the range of your eyes can reach

A canvas made of snow
extended in the forest
mother and daughter are
two colorful moving strokes

An army of trees
standing in curvy white surface
waiting patiently for a human to show up
maybe an animal instead

Life frozen among these
dry trees. Truth stays
underneath

Midnight
wind singing outside the window
I sing with keyboard

Layered sky

layered by coloured clouds

cars are moving ants underneath

A road, long and straight

towards the end of the sky

we'll never reach the end

Trees stand along both sides

telling an old story through centuries

without a single word

Silence inside the car

her light snore from backseat

makes more silence

Five hours is not long to a day

to a half day

it's an all

You complained

"No time!"

use the time for complaining

"Life is not easy and pretty" she said
smile or cry, angry or happy
one way or the other, you should try"

She's on the other side of the line
stressed out, how could I
hug her skin to skin

Mommy is leaving today

wake up at 3am

room is full of darkness

Drifting far from a river of mind

floating safely in Jesus hands

on Good Friday

Finally, spring is here
if you don't believe, look at
teen girls' bare legs

When winter doesn't want to go away
spring lives in my
yellow blooming daffodil pot

How can I fill this emptiness

before she leaves, where

I see her white hair

Rain is knocking the window

I close the curtain

for hearing it clearly

Mother, daughter,husband
love equals to responsibility
in everyday life

Finish editing the fourth one
unknown publisher
is still unknown

Sleeplessness

may cure loneliness

thoughts are companions

A group of ten years

gains appetite and wisdom every other week,

when Bible is with us

White hair covered
she smiles like a little girl
when her girl is facing her
I'm the girl

Ladies and gentlemen
laughter and tears
in a wechat poetry group

Woke up at 3am
no moon, light
was from a prayer

Two three words
enough for a heart
melt or broken

We walked on a snow covered path

face frozen, but

lips carried stories

It's not a joke

when time passes by

you earn wrinkles and sigh

Uncountable wisdom is on these shelves

none is mine, but a first page

is born on my keyboard, right now

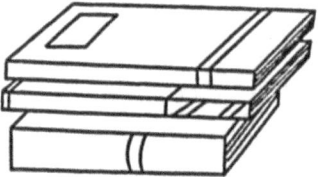

"From this, I see a Great writer in the future"

after he read this freshly-finished novel

this sentence will repeat thousands times

in my days

Way too much
guests and parties
when you own a lonely heart

Guilty, last 2 months
25000 words only,
a sign of lazinese or slow thinker
forgiveness is not easy to give inwards

In closet, on floor, I write
hiding light and typing sound
from the sleeping world

Empty
nothing in time
including dreams

White cover seals up the world

temperature underneath

is as deep as a heart

A tree tip out there carries my floating heart

clear window in front

divides body and mind

Racing heart and shaky hands
a mystery in mid-afternoon
a love storm to believe or a lab test?

Tme has been edited
the sixth book
will talk

If I love

the destination is you

this life and next life

Even they are two books now

you and I

were on the same page

The first love
one seed in heart
a full garden it grows

Sunny weekend
cleans our shoes for a journey
on a road and in mind

Uncountable wisdom is on these shelves
none is mine, but a first page is born
on my keyboard, right now

Melancholy dawn
a chirping bird
suddenly stopped chirping

Back to writing

when a story starts

emptiness is filled with words

Missing you

is a habbit, it's nothing to do

with your age

I touched petals and soil

under a cloudless sky

with tears nobody can see

Overtired

sleep is not a solution

anymore

When something comes to mind
with keyboard I mark it down
"something" is everywhere
in every moment to mind

A day for children
full of laughters and screams
on Ziplines and parents' hearts

Dry like sand of desert
my brain is losing
enthusiasm of writing

Almost half a year gone
a plan is not finished
close to a half

7 kilometers

gone with breeze

under my running feet

Far behind my writting plan

A voice is whispering:

Can you find yourself anymore?

Stuck in the middle of

writting

and real life

If somebody asks me

what do you want at this moment

answer is:"A life without internet!"

How can I enter my story
in an electronic world
"self control" is the key

Sitting beside me
a warm body with temperature
once in my womb now a teacher of English
grammar

10K under a pair of running feet

I gain back

my hips, ankles and knees

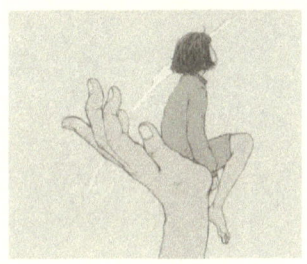

When the rain washing the earth

cleansing milk for my thought

is a day dream

Ready to go
from north to norther
Iceberg will whiten my heart

Back pain
makes a day
much longer

Literature Awards
Lit up the night
Dawn is not far

Woke up at 2am
There was a big party
In my quiet soul

Back to library

a place with discipline

is a start for a marching mind

Birds are chirping

around a winter-like mind

to announce a true spring

Shaking candle flame
on the desk
wind blows from my heart

If only one word I need
"tranquillity"
will be

Alive again
when September is here
harvest is near

The distance from a heart
to her own body
could be far

Summer shows off her warm skin tone

when Fall dyed his leaves

into brown, yellow and red

Water flows over my fingers

If you don't believe

ask my piano

Abandoned, by your own mind
when everyday filled with responsibilities
you turned into a slave of other's mind

My sun is shinning
whenever your face
carries smile

Body sings in winter
mind cries for a summer
spirit travels into a new year

Editing my Haiku poetry
the dim lamp light
is my partner

99 years on earth

Up there now

Billy Graham

An old plant sits on a book shelf

telling a story in winter

about green lives

Hibernate in twitter and Facebook

wake up

from Wechat

A whirlpool

jets from different directions

I drown into Wechat

A father in bed
curled his body like a baby
on Father's day

Birds singing outside the window
rhythmed snoring on bed
a symphony on the morning of Father's day

Birds singing outside
I sing inside
on a laptop

Where are you?
a drought garden sighed
raindrops came suddenly

A lecture about Tai Chi
opened 200 pairs of ears
on a western land

Black and white, Yin and Yang
in two fish eyes
conclude the universe

Giving is better than receiving

a ruler for you and me

from Bible

After a nightmare

I keened down beside the bed

praying

A patch of weed-like carpet flowers
as golden as the morning sun
under my feet

A bee sings a bee song
a girl stopped running and stared at a flower
in my dream

Morning sunlight squeezed in

Filled my eyes with hope

Of another prospective day

A choir in a tree

wakes me up every morning

3 different types of birds are my neighbours

When you expect too much

Disappointment will be more

It's a fact, not a sagacious motto

Summer heat

takes off her clothes

a naked woman standing in a dream

Many people around you
in fact, they are
real strangers

If you want to laugh
just laugh
open your chest and soul

An ant crawling on the countertop

it's a sign

of a true summer

Carpet made of pink flower pedals

telling a story of

the short life of a peony

It's not a fairy tale anymore
two men, a woman and a child
a polyamorous family

She came back from an eastern country
"Interesting" was the word
to describe "black and white"

Facing a forest
green is all
in eyes and heart

A girl in an exam
a mother waiting in a car
time walks quietly

Leaves dancing on the tips of the tree

invisible wind

is the director behind the show

No cloud

my heart is like the blue sky

stay deep

Don't tell anyone
hlied to the group of strangers
on purpose

If I need to give you a name
magical Dragon
will be

A show

an actress living a life on the stage

you are the stage light

If a heart can be split into two rivers

I'd like to give one to you

from a shower head

A wide river
between two hearts
no bridge to cross

Summer sun
kisses her lips
when she stops talking

The fiction
turned into a true story
after the thumb was up

To be honest to yourself
or not to be
is not a question but an answer

Sadness, sorrow

on a raining day

is from the inside of a heart

Judgement is from

a female tree

if I am allowed to give her a gender

Bellows blows hurricane

From a cut

Of a thumb

Don't hold the flow

when emotion travels

in your blood

Freedom bursts out

when a housewife laughs

in the midnight

Don't be afraid

even a rain of criticism

pouring from the sky

You can't hear birds' songs

during the bright day

since other noises covered up

One leaf falls

then another follows

heart stops pounding

He gives you the talent
when He planned
to use you

Dragon boat day
a sticky dumpling
refused to be cooked

Sweat

came from a heart

working out too hard

Haiku cries out

musical notes

in a car

I'd like to borrow a hat
when there is no umbrella
to borrow

Young faces diminished
when those bare legs
showed up

No need to challenge yourself

when you are facing

the strong wind

A stop sign

stops

a poem

Waked up in the car
kids came out of the school
the bell was late

If you don't know the answer
ask the dictionary
and shut your mouth

One shaking tree
on the empty field
facing a lonely car

Surrounded by noises
eyes filled with people
she sits there along

A pigeon lands on the roof
staring at me, probably
it's me staring at her

Blond hair and blue eyes
you pass by me like a stranger
in fact, I am a stranger

A morning without a phone

is a paradise

for a writer

A river of Haiku

flows into the future

in a sunny morning

Don't say it

before you can do it

dawn is the time when sun comes up

Green Orchard

a rare color joined in

my life

Morality

becomes shit

when true feelings appear

Oracle talks in ancient language

I walk on the turtle shell

read a scholar's mind

If a B can be presented
give it to somebody
you don't care

A snow storm
came from a voice message
at midnight

A summary of China Lake
at rest under the down quilt
outside the window, 36 degree minus
just like my brain frozen and clean

Shaking nonstop
flesh and heart, hope and happiness
grows into an invisible zone
what's the magic cloak?